Fence & Gate Ideas

CREATIVE
PUBLISHING
international

CHANHASSEN, MINNESOTA

www.creativepub.com

CONTENTS

WHAT MAKES A GREAT FENCE OR GATE?

A great fence serves the practical purposes you want it to, such as providing privacy, climate control and security, while also enhancing the aesthetic beauty of the entire outdoor area. The type and architectural style of the fence will influence its impact on the surrounding environment. A great fence creates the visual impact you were striving for; whether that's a traditional, Colonial white picket fence that adds an all-American feel, or a rustic split rail that adds an old-fashioned Western flavor; and still performs the practical function it was built for, such as defining boundaries or providing privacy.

Fences and gates can make your yard more usable by transforming it into a more effectively and efficiently used space. A great fence can provide a multitude of functions, both practical and decorative, but it will usually have one primary purpose. For example, when used in a practical application, fences can be used to define boundaries, protect property and provide privacy.

In a decorative capacity, they act as an attractive background for plants, serve as a visual point of interest in a landscape and complement the architectural design of a home's exterior. Fences set the tone in an outdoor setting and influence the visual impact of the area that lies within them. A great fence can transform an ordinary, open yard into an attractive, secure retreat from the outside world.

A Portfolio of Fence & Gate Ideas is here to guide you as you plan and make decisions about the design of your fence and gate. You'll find information to help you determine why you want to build a fence and the functions you need it to perform. You'll find a range of fence styles to help you decide which fence type and materials will work best for your fence and gate design. *A Portfolio of Fence & Gate Ideas* showcases some of the most creative and innovative ideas for integrating these multifunctional fences and gates into your landscape or yard.

Photo courtesy of Walpole Woodworkers Inc.

Photo courtesy of Cy DeCosse Inc.

This pretty picket fence frames the front of this yard, as well as the front of this house, creating an enchanting and inviting entrance. The pointed white pickets and the scalloped shape, formed by the graduated lengths, enhance the Victorian style of the house and add a taste of tradition.

A tall, solid board fence *creates a secluded sanctuary and provides privacy for an outdoor area. An attractive lattice border is attached to the top of the fence. The open lattice addition extends the height of the fence, but keeps it from feeling too confining. On the interior side of the fence, lush green plants use the natural wood of the fence panels as an attractive backdrop, while colorful flowering plants fill the open area on the upper portion of the fence.*

This rustic post-and-rail fence is one of the oldest and most widely used fence designs. The open design uses less lumber than other fence types, making it a logical choice for holding a herd of livestock or enclosing large areas of land, such as rural farmland.

Planning

WHAT DO FENCES & GATES DO?

Fences and gates do so much more than mark a boundary. Fences and gates can transform an outdoor area in many ways. They protect and enhance our properties by defining the perimeters and forming a frame around the area within. They can transform your yard into an extension of your living area that is an attractive, secure retreat from the outside world.

The first step in determining which type of fence or gate is best for you is to ask yourself— what you want your fence or gate to do? Some of the most common reasons for building fences and gates include; marking boundaries, creating privacy, providing protection, controlling noise, wind and sunlight.

In a decorative capacity, fences and gates can be used to enhance the look of your property.

They can be integrated into a landscape to add character to an outdoor setting, or to reflect the architectural style of a home. Be sure to consider the aesthetic impact a fence or gate will have on the surrounding environment, and coordinate your design so that it is in harmony with existing elements in the outdoor area.

Before you make your final decisions, take a look at the fences and gates in your surrounding neighborhood. Study the materials and styles, particularly of houses similar to yours, and try to imagine if they are right for your yard. You can customize an ordinary fence or gate design and give it an original look by incorporating interesting elements, such as decorative fence tops, fencing patterns and unusual shapes, such as curves and arches, into the design.

Subtle design differences in the gate panel and a small overhead arbor designate the entrance and highlight the transition from one outdoor environment to another. Climbing plants soften the look and increase the intimacy and sense of privacy.

An ornamental fence of wrought iron and brick adds a classic touch and a feeling of formality to this outdoor area. The low fence defines the perimeter of the property, and the open design of the iron pickets keeps the area from feeling too confined.

PROVIDE PRIVACY & PROTECTION

Fences and gates are the perfect way to increase the privacy in an outdoor setting. Fences increase privacy by surrounding an area with a solid, sturdy barrier which deters unwelcome invasions of privacy. The most effective privacy fences are those you can't see over, under, around, or through. They block views and control access into your yard. If you are planning to add a privacy fence, make sure the fence design you choose won't give the setting a boxed-in feel.

Fences also keep people, especially small children, away from potential hazards, like swimming pools. Many

Vinyl-coated chain-link gives this fence a green color which allows it to blend smoothly into its surroundings. This type of fence is an inexpensive way to keep animals and kids in the yard without visually intruding on the natural landscape.

Many building codes require fences around pools. The protective picket fence that surrounds this backyard pool keeps the area safe and secluded. The scalloped fence top and large double gate add a delightfully decorative touch.

Visual interest and privacy are provided by combining two different fence designs. The elegant lattice creates a decorative and airy screen, while the louvered panel provides privacy and wind protection.

building codes require fences around swimming pools to protect children and nonswimmers from unsupervised access to the pool area. Fences can also be used to protect children and pets by keeping them safe inside an area, such as a play yard or kennel. Chain link and wire mesh are excellent materials for play yard fences—the open design allows parents to keep an eye on their children while they are safely inside the fenced area. Wire mesh is similar to chain link, but thinner and lighter. Fences for higher security should be sturdier and harder to climb than wire mesh or

chain link. The most effective are those that use vertical boards or plywood panels.

Pet owners are also responsible for containing their animals. Most dogs can dig under fences, and larger dogs can break through a flimsy fence. Chain link, heavy wire, or solid panels set in concrete are good solutions. Metal fencing is preferable to wood because it is not damaged by scratching and gnawing. In rural areas, fences are needed to keep livestock from straying. Livestock fences are usually post-and-rail, or barbed wire.

DEFINE BOUNDARIES & ESTABLISH ACTIVITY AREAS

Fences that define boundaries also help organize the landscape and give it visual definition. Fences are used to establish property lines and mark boundaries. You can use fences and gates to shape and define specific areas of use, such as those that seclude and protect recreation and relaxation areas around pools and patios. Fences can also surround and hide storage and compost areas, and frame and define vegetable and flower gardens. Fences and gates can be used to line the perimeter of your property, separating private from public spaces.

If you don't want to feel enclosed by your fence, low or open types of fences physically separate areas, yet visually preserve the openness and overall size of the yard. Taller fences can help hide unattractive sights, such as trash or service areas. You can get more privacy with a chain link by inserting thin slats of plastic or wood through the links. The slats are commercially available, and designed specifically for this purpose.

Photo courtesy of Walpole Woodworkers Inc.

*A **vibrant variation** of a classic picket fence defines this front yard, without obstructing the view.*

*A **tall, solid board fence** extends the activity area to the side of this house and keeps the area separate and secluded from the more public areas of the yard. The lattice top adds a romantic charm and keeps the fence from feeling too confining to those within.*

Photo courtesy of California Redwood Association

(above) **The handsome perimeter fence** *that surrounds this property does so much more than mark boundaries. It adds privacy, creates a backdrop for a garden and enhances the entire outdoor area.*

(left) **The decorative iron picket** *offers strength and beauty, as well as an air of distinction. The fence defines the private yard area and separates it from the public boulevard area in the front of the house. The open design of the fence establishes the boundary without disturbing the visual continuity of the landscape.*

CONTROL CLIMATE & BUFFER NOISE

Fences help buffer street noise, barking dogs and noisy neighbors. You can control noise by placing fences at strategic locations around a yard. When it comes to blocking noise, the thicker and higher the barrier, the more effective it will be. Solid panel fences are able to mute and deflect a good deal of noise. Other types of fences are not as effective at controlling noise. Fences can also affect the amount of noise you think you hear, by blocking the visual source of noise.

Fences can also help control the environment by altering the effects of wind or sunlight, and creating microclimates within a yard. A microclimate is a small area in a landscape that has a different climactic condition. The climates in these localized areas can be altered by controlling the amounts of sunlight and wind. You can use fences to filter the sun's glare and transform a strong wind into a comfortable breeze.

To effectively control the effects of elements such as wind and sunlight within your yard, you'll have to study the impact they have on your property, then plan your fence design and location accordingly. For example, solid barriers provide little protection from the wind across large expanses of yard—the wind simply goes right over the fence. A fence with an open design, such as spaced boards, slats, louvers or woven lath, breaks up a steady wind into smaller breezes. Therefore, this type of fence is more effective in protecting large open areas from strong winds.

Decorative fence panels *are strategically positioned to create an effective windbreak. While the lattice tops are a charming touch, they also increase the windbreaking capabilities of the fence.*

Lattice panels *provide the perfect windbreak for an open, windswept expanse. The open weave of the lattice breaks a gust of wind into small, buffered breezes.*

An attractive lattice screen *turns a sunny patio into a quiet comfortable play area. The open design of the lattice allows sunlight to filter through and breaks strong winds to light breezes.*

ENHANCE THE AMBIENCE

The addition of a fence or gate can enhance the aesthetic appearance of your property. A well-designed and well-crafted fence or gate can be a strikingly beautiful addition to a yard. Even a fence with a fairly simple structure will have a strong visual impact and play a significant role in the visual impression your property creates. A fence or gate will give you a positive return on investment as well as a pleasant place to enjoy the outdoor environment.

In addition to their functional role, fences have many aesthetic qualities as well. They can support vines and climbing plants and serve as natural backgrounds for planting beds and outdoor lighting effects. The color and texture of a fence should complement the surrounding elements—dark fences contrast with light foliage and blooms, while brightly colored flowers have a striking appearance when backed by a light-colored fence.

Photo courtesy of Walpole Woodworkers Inc.

Adding a scalloped top to an ordinary board fence gives this fence a charming, old-fashioned appeal.

Photo courtesy of Champlain Stone, Ltd.

This distinct combination of natural stone and white picket is a reflection of the style and grace that can be achieved with proper planning. This decorative fence not only serves the function of defining this front yard, it also adds a charming character and beauty to this hilltop homestead.

Photo courtesy of Walpole Woodworkers Inc.

(above) **A subtle distinction in design,** *such as the scalloped top of this gate, is one way to differentiate a gate opening from the rest of the fence.*

(right) **A painted redwood fence, gate and overhead arbor** *combine to create an outdoor foyer that provides privacy and personality for the yard. The widely spaced lattice creates an attractive fence that defines the yard without isolating it.*

Photo courtesy of California Redwood Association

*A **solid privacy fence** helps keep the windows on this side of the house shaded and the inside cool. The tall fence creates a private and secluded alcove along a previously unused side of the house.*

Planning

LOCATION OF A FENCE

The function you want your fence or gate to perform, and the physical characteristics of the site itself, will be determining factors in deciding where to locate a fence. Your goal is to locate a fence where it will do the job you want it to do. Decide what things in your yard you want to change or camouflage, and what things cannot be changed and will need to be worked around, such as a sloping hillside.

Planning in advance helps you estimate materials and allows you to conceptualize the whole project ahead of time so you can experiment with various ideas. Begin by imagining a fence or gate in various locations around your yard. Try to picture how it will alter the physical characteristics of the setting. For example, a fence that blocks a window for privacy will also affect the amount of sunlight that enters the house. All fence projects,

large or small, should be planned and drawn out before you begin, on paper or on a computer.

Survey the actual site where the fence will be built. Look at the way traffic flows around the setting and think about how wide the openings need to be to accommodate that traffic. Consider where fences around activity areas are located and what types of activities these areas are used for. Take into account lot size, shape and grade, as well as the orientation of the sun, the direction of the wind and the characteristics of surrounding structures and plantings.

You'll need to determine the location of the gate within the fence. The most logical locations are places where the fence intersects with a drive or walkway. Make sure the gate opening can accommodate the foot traffic and machinery that need to pass through it.

Fences within fences. *A tall privacy fence defines the perimeter of the yard and protects the privacy of this poolside patio area. A short, widely spaced board fence separates the front yard from the back and provides a safety barrier around the pool area.*

17

BUILDING CODES & REQUIREMENTS

Two important aspects to consider when building a fence are building codes and property lines. Many communities have building codes that define basic design and construction requirements for fencing. For example, there may be ordinances limiting the height of fences around yards or located near traffic intersections. Maximum fence height is usually limited to six to eight feet. Fence materials are also regulated in some areas. Your local building department or planning office is the best source of current information about local codes, laws and

restrictions. Check with these offices before starting a fence project.

It is always a good idea to advise your neighbors of your intentions to build a fence. You both should confirm the exact location of your property lines to determine the correct setback distance. The setback distance is the legal distance any structure must be from an adjacent property line. The setback distance is determined by the local building code, and prevents you from building your fence too close to property lines.

Obey local setback regulations *when planning fences. The setback distance is the distance you must keep between your fence and your neighbor's property line. Your community inspections office will have current information about setback regulations and about any other restrictions on how and where you can build a fence or other landscape structures.*

setback distance

property line

(left) **Involve your neighbors** as you make your plans to build a fence. Make sure they do not object to your plans and will be comfortable with the effects the fence will have on their property.

(bottom) **These low, openly spaced pickets** create an attractive front yard fence that won't obstruct views.

FENCE MATERIALS

Fences and gates can be made of a wide range of different materials. In this section you'll find examples of fences made of wood, as well as of vinyl, metal, glass, stone and masonry materials. And, even though the majority of fences are built partially or completely out of wood, much of the information, including design and layout considerations, can be applied to fences constructed from other types of materials.

Wood is the most popular fencing material because it is so versatile. This can be seen in the variety of fence types available in wood designs, such as split rails, grapestakes, pickets, lattice and many more. The style or look of wood fencing ranges from the rustic natural look of split rails, to the more formal appearance of straight-cut corners and smooth, flat, painted pickets.

If you want to maintain the natural look of a wood fence, use pressure-treated lumber that has been chemically treated to resist decay, or a decay-resistant wood, such as cedar or redwood, and let the wood age naturally. These woods turn an attractive shade of silvery gray when exposed to the weather. If the lumber you use isn't naturally resistant to decay, or you want to preserve the natural look of cedar or redwood, use a clear sealer.

There are a number of finishes you can apply to protect a wood fence or gate. Stain, paint and clear sealers offer the best results. Any applied finish will need to be reapplied annually to preserve the original color or look of the wood. Paint is an excellent wood preservative; it seals and protects wood surfaces. Semitransparent stains allow wood grain to show, while heavier stains cover wood grain but not texture. Clear sealers help prevent rain and moisture from soaking into the wood.

A variety of preassembled wood panels is available to simplify construction of fences. Preassembled panels include (from left to right): lattice panels, solid panels with lattice tops, staggered board, horizontal board, modified picket and dog-eared board. Preassembled gates are also available to match many panel styles. Because of the predetermined size, there are limitations to the use of panels as a fencing material.

(left) **A delightfully detailed** *wooden fence has been finished with a light tan stain that gives the fence a more refined and formal appeal. The scalloped cut of the fence top is accentuated by the scalloped design of the rail.*

(right) **A solid board fence of weather-resistant redwood** *divides and provides privacy for this beautiful backyard garden. Custom latticework on the fence top adds a refined elegance and gives you a glimpse of the view on the other side.*

Wire, metal & iron

Metal, iron and especially wire are, second to wood, some of the most versatile fence materials. Metal materials can be incorporated as part of a wood fence design, or they can be used to create an all-metal fence. Wire for outdoor fencing is made of galvanized steel and comes in a number of gauges. It is sometimes coated with polyester or vinyl. Chain link is one example of wire fencing. Wire and other metal fences can provide security, support plants and vines, enclose play yards and animal pens and protect garden areas from foot traffic and small animals.

To many, ornamental fencing means the wrought-iron fencing that was commonly found gracing the mansions of the Victorian era. Today, ornamental fencing not only includes traditional wrought iron, but ornamental steel and aluminum as well. Designs in metal fencing range from ornate handcrafted works of art to sleek modern grillwork. The visual results of ornamental fencing can be very dramatic, but this material is costly and difficult to install. It's best to consult with someone who specializes in ornamental metal fences if you are considering a job this complex. Prefabricated sections of metal fencing make it easier to install an ornamental fence yourself.

A decorative steel picket fence adds a feeling of old-world gracefulness, as well as quality and durability. There is a wide array of decorative options available, making it easy to mix and match to create the ultimate ornamental fence design. For example, the stately finials featured on this fence are an option that adds distinction.

(above) **An ornamental painted wrought-iron fence** *provides protection and security for this backyard pool and patio area. The close spacing of the iron pickets in this fence design keeps kids from wandering unsupervised into the pool area, while the visual openness of the design offers a clear view of the entire area from both inside and outside the fence.*

(left) **This conventional chain-link fence** *keeps pets and kids restricted to the safety of the yard. The open design of the fence material keeps the fenced-in area from feeling too confining, and doesn't block the view.*

VINYL, GLASS & PLASTIC

Vinyl fencing is available in many of the same styles as traditional wood fencing—post-and-rail, post-and-board, basketweave, picket and others. Many of the tools and techniques used to install wood fencing are used to install a vinyl fence, as well. Once installed, vinyl fences are easy to maintain because they're resistant to cracking, rotting, chipping or rusting, and they never need painting.

Transparent materials, such as glass and plastic, admit the maximum amount of light and offer a clear view, while providing wind protection in small areas, such as patios and decks. In larger areas, any solid barrier, such as glass or plastic, will be relatively ineffective in blocking wind.

Glass is more suitable than plastic in some situations because of its high resistance to abrasion, but not recommended for use in high-activity or high-traffic areas, where glass poses a safety threat. If you are considering a glass fence or screen, consult a professional before beginning. The supporting structure for a glass fence panel must be rigid so that the glass cannot be twisted, which causes breakage. The fence structure must also be designed to flex with the expansion and contraction of the glass.

The beauty of vinyl fencing is more than skin deep. The nostalgic ambience and old-fashioned beauty give this vinyl fence a turn-of-the-century charm, without the traditional maintenance.

(above) **A variety of vinyl fence styles** are featured in this well-coordinated backyard assembly. With white vinyl fencing, the ambience you create is always fresh, clean and bright.

(left) **The vinyl fence** that surrounds the pool brings the beauty of a traditional white fence—without the work. The maintenance-free vinyl is the perfect fencing material to pair with the red brick used for the base of the wall. Both materials have a formal appeal and are made from materials that will last a lifetime.

MASONRY & OTHER FENCE MATERIALS

Masonry materials, such as brick and concrete, and natural stone and rock are some of the other materials that can be used to build effective fences. Building a fence out of masonry materials, such as brick, requires specialized masonry techniques; be sure to consult a contractor if you are considering installing a fence of this kind.

Masonry and natural stone materials are useful fencing materials for many situations.

For example, a tall poured concrete fence is a highly effective noise barrier. Natural fieldstone can be used to build a rustic-looking fence that is both strong and attractive. And a high fence made of brick also offers privacy and security. A masonry fence made of brick adds a natural warmth and character to an outdoor area. Brick fences work well with existing brick elements, such as patios, to give the entire area an upscale and formal appeal.

A beautiful brick fence winds its way along one edge of this formal garden area. This dynamic fence design is tall enough to create an effective boundary, but low enough to allow full enjoyment of the parklike setting.

Photo courtesy of Brick Institute of America

(left) **Decorative block** *adds visual interest to a plain concrete block wall. This creative construction application gives an ordinary cinder-block fence an interesting visual appeal.*

This rustic-looking stone veneer fence *adds a rugged flavor to an outdoor setting. Natural stone fences are both sturdy and solid. Stone veneer cemented to a cinder-block wall copies the look of a natural stone fence, at a fraction of the cost.*

Decorative concrete block *also may be used to build an entire wall. Concrete block is inexpensive and available in decorative and plain styles. This decorative block pattern features an open design that lightens the look of the heavy concrete.*

Design

TYPES OF FENCES

When choosing what type of fence to install, ask yourself: what type of fence best fits the surrounding landscape and architecture? Variations in materials, sizes and shapes create different fence and gate styles and designs. You can also combine different types of fence materials, such as wood and stone, to create distinctive fence designs. The basic elements of fence framework (posts, rails and siding or wire), remain the same, no matter what style is chosen.

Posts are the vertical upright portions of the fence. The posts support the horizontal rails, which are sometimes called stringers. Siding is the exterior material that is attached to the rails. There are many options available in siding materials—from plain, flat boards, to woven lattice or rustic grapestakes. Prefabricated panels of entire fence sections are also available. These panels make installing a solid board fence much easier and less time-consuming. However, there are limitations with fence panels. Because they come in predetermined sizes and styles, panels are not the best choice in every situation.

The overall appearance of your fence will depend not only on the basic style you've chosen, but also on the materials used in its construction; its actual dimensions, such as height and post spacing; and the characteristics of the surrounding property. All of these elements must work in harmony to form a functional and attractive fence or gate structure.

This beautiful brick fence is an example of a fence that does not have the typical post-and-rail framework. Even so, the shape of the fence and the latticelike brickwork resemble the visual effect of traditional post-and-rail fence construction.

(above) **The natural look of split-rail fencing** *gives this yard an authentic old-fashioned appearance. This sturdy fence is a practical answer to many fencing needs, such as defining boundaries. Post-and-rail fences can easily be tailored to run along the uneven contours of your terrain.*

POST & RAIL

The original post-and-rail fence was a split-rail fence design. Post-and-rail fences are well suited for enclosing large areas of land because they use less wood than other types of fencing. They are often used in rural settings to contain livestock or to serve as boundary markers. Post-and-rail fences are even used as a decorative fencing style when a rustic flavor is desired in a landscape. These fences are one solution for those who want a border around their yard but don't want to block the view. A stacked split-rail fence is a beautiful variation of the traditional version. This type of fence is made by stacking rails in a simple zigzag line. No posts are required to build a stacked split-rail fence, so they are ideal for use in rocky terrains.

Not all post-and-rail fences are rustic-looking; they can be built with cleanly cut 2 x 6 rails and 4 x 4 posts and painted white, to give them a very formal look. Post-and-rail fences are also available in vinyl versions. Mortised post-and-rail fences are another variation of the original. Two of the most common methods of mortising rails into posts are achieved by overlapping the rails or cutting tenons into the rail ends.

(above) **The smooth, graceful curve** *of this post-and-rail fence shows how flexible and adaptable to the terrain this type of fencing can be. The length of the rails can be custom-cut to accommodate tricky maneuvers, like the one shown here, and changes in the grade.*

(right) **This cedar split-rail fence** *represents one of the easiest fencing styles to build. In this particular post-and-rail design, the rails are mortised into the poles for a rustic-looking fence with a more formal appeal.*

(above) ***A zigzag fence of rustic split rails*** *is an example of typical early pioneer fencing. These fences were popular, especially in areas with rocky terrain, because they were easy to build and involved no posts, so no digging was required.*

(below) ***A formal-looking post-and-rail fence*** *features double driveway gates and tall, impressive pillars. The unique texture and color of the concrete pillars and fence posts add a simple elegance to this fence and entry.*

Rugged and ready to work, this split-rail fence is strengthened by diagonal braces attached to the outside of the posts. The entrance is announced by a tall post that has a sphere-shaped top, which is known as a finial.

Design

POST & RAIL

Post-and-board fences are a simple variation that evolved from post-and-rail fences when advancements in technology created machines that made it possible to cut boards for fencing and gate materials directly at the site.

A typical post-and-board fence is very similar in design to a post-and-rail fence, except the rails are boards that are attached to the sides of square posts, rather than mortised into the center of the post, as in post-and-rail fences. There are a number of post-and-board fence designs that are decorative variations and embellishments of the basic post-and-board design. These post-and-board variations have practical functions in addition to adding visual interest. For example, post-and-board designs that feature closely spaced boards, like picket fences, or alternating boards that overlap vertically on opposite sides, like board-on-board fences, will keep toddlers and pets from getting through the fence. The size of the boards and posts you use will depend on your fence design. Like post-and-rail fences, post-and-board fence designs use less lumber than any other fence style, and they adapt well to rolling terrain.

A square-edged version of a traditional post-and-rail fence, called a post-and-board, is a popular livestock and farmland fencing style. In this fence style, flat, square-edged boards are attached to one side of the rail, which gives this fence a handsome design that has smooth surfaces and balanced proportions.

This painted post-and-rail fence captures the look of a Kentucky horse farm and creates an image of a leisurely life and simple sophistication.

This variation of a post-and-board fence features double-sided posts with the board sandwiched in between. Boards that run diagonally from one corner of a fence section to another form a repeating crisscross design within the fence. The large posts are topped with flat, square decorative finials.

BOARD

A board fence begins with the basic frame of a traditional post-and-board fence, which has at least two rails that run parallel with the ground and are attached to one side of the vertical posts. Board fences can be designed and built in a number of different variations. Pickets, alternating boards, horizontal patterns, louvers, grapestakes and basketweave fences are just some of the most common variations.

Siding is usually attached to the frame in a vertical pattern rather than a horizontal pattern, such as the way pickets are attached. Your fence siding should reach from below the bottom rail to the top rail, with at least 2 inches between the bottom of the fence and the ground; this protects the wood from constant contact with moisture from the ground and accommodates the expansion and contraction of the ground due to freezing and thawing. You can extend the siding material above the top rail for additional height or for a special visual effect.

Board fence designs that include closely spaced boards, or overlapping boards on alternating sides, will keep toddlers and pets from slipping through the fence. Diagonal board patterns and prefabricated fence panels are also decorative board fence options.

A rustic, yet contemporary, grapestake fence provides security and privacy in this front yard. For a creative contrast, brick columns frame a redwood gate and create an impressive entryway.

This flattering fence design *features two variations of board-style fencing—a solid board fence with a cap makes up the lower half of the fence, while a delicate open lattice is used on the upper portion. The square edges of the lattice combine with the graceful curve on the top of the fence for a stunning effect.*

BOARD

Many board fence designs feature boards nailed to one side of the post-and-rail frame, which results in a fence that has a front side and a back side. There are many ways you can change or enhance the look of a fence. One popular solution is a board fence that looks good on both sides—often referred to as "a good-neighbor fence." An example of a good-neighbor fence is a staggered board fence; the boards are attached to both sides of the frame so the fence looks good from either side, which is likely to please your neighbors.

Louvered fences are a relatively expensive board fence design because they require more material per foot than a solid board fence of the same height. Louvered fences can have either vertical or horizontal louvers. The louvers provide privacy without completely blocking airflow. Depending on the direction of the louvers (horizontal or vertical), spacing and angle, you can control sunlight, calm harsh winds or completely block the view from outside into a yard. With either type of louvered fence, the edge of one louver must overlap the edge of the next one to provide privacy.

A simple inset board fence *encloses this patio. The solid fence is just high enough to provide privacy without giving the space a feeling of confinement.*

This board-on-board fence is a good example of a good-neighbor fence because it creates a fully enclosed fence surface and a finished appearance on both sides. This type of fence also offers a great deal of privacy, and the configuration allows gentle breezes to filter through.

The basic frame of a classic post-and-board fence becomes part of the visual design of one side of this solid board fence.

BOARD VARIATIONS

One variation of the basic board fence is a horizontal or a vertical basketweave design. A basketweave fence has a pleasing interwoven design that casts an attractive shadow pattern. Basketweave fences are fairly easy to construct. You only need to use one thin post, or spacer, for each section, which makes weaving the thinly cut boards much easier. Because the spacers and boards are cut much thinner for this design, these fences use less siding material than a typical board fence.

Picket fences are board fences that are often associated with Colonial architecture. Today picket fences are found with almost any type of house, in both the city and the country. The classic picket fence is about three feet high. There are a number of different picket and post designs available that you can use to give your fence an individual character and still maintain the feeling of a traditional picket fence design.

Some variations of a picket fence include the classic pointed-top picket design, varying the heights and widths of the pickets; tightly spaced and contoured pickets; and thick pickets. Shaped tops are one way to give a distinctive look to a picket fence. Using pickets of different lengths creates a scalloped effect. Lumber dealers and fence suppliers don't always carry ready-made pickets, but you may find them at a home center, or have the lumberyard cut them for you. You can also cut the picket top designs yourself or have a cabinet shop or woodworker do the work.

A beautiful, solid board fence surrounds this secluded setting, *and guides visitors to the grandeur of the delightful arched gateway. This enchanting entrance is enhanced by the attractive lattice top treatment. The rounded door completes the look of this charming entry.*

Photo courtesy of California Redwood Association

Photo courtesy of Walpole Woodworkers Inc.

This classic grapestake fence creates a rustic atmosphere and provides complete privacy.

Photo courtesy of Southern Pine Council

This board-on-board fence will be seen from both sides within this outdoor setting, and the well-planned design of the fence reflects this. This design has boards attached so they are staggered on opposite sides of the rails. This way, the fence looks good from both sides.

ADDITIONAL TYPES OF FENCES

Traditionally, the majority of fences were made partially or entirely out of wood. Today, there are many types of fencing to choose from, in addition to the traditional wood fences. Wire mesh and chain link are types of fences that are essentially post-and-rail fences that use metal or steel materials for the posts, rails and siding. Both wire mesh and chain-link fences are easy to maintain and are good choices for many security purposes.

Ornamental iron is a sophisticated and classic fencing material. Because ornamental fences have a very formal appearance, they require the right setting to be effective. Iron fences come in a variety of styles, from tall, vertical designs to curving, rolling fences, which are all based on a traditonal post-and-board fence design. Many are metal versions of a classic picket design. These fences don't offer much visual privacy, but they provide good protection and security, if the space between bars is small enough.

Solid fences are often made of masonry, brick or natural stone. Masonry fences are basically panel fences that are made up of one solid, continous panel. These types of fences are sometimes considered garden walls.

(right) **Natural fieldstone** *makes an excellent material for a low garden fence. The natural color and texture of the stones are a natural complement to any outdoor setting.*

An ornamental aluminum fence is constructed in a classic post-and-board style. The metal material adds to the atmosphere of elegance in this poolside setting. This fancy fence not only enhances the overall ambience of the area, it provides a safe protective barrier around the pool.

Glass and canvas are two other materials you might consider for panel fencing options. A glass fence will preserve a view or even create the feeling of a room outside. However, even when the most careful precautions are taken, a glass fence is susceptible to damage from vandalism or accidental breakage. Canvas used in a panel fence design emits a fresh, casual feel and provides privacy. These types of panel fences are great for beach houses or outdoor settings in the city.

As you can see, in addition to wood, there are a number of effective fencing materials that can be applied to a standard type of fence, such as a post-and-rail or board fence. You can combine different fencing materials, such as brick and wood, to create a traditional type of fencing, such as a post-and-board design that uses brick for the post material and wood for the boards. These combination fences are effective options when you want to make a more dramatic impression than you would be able to achieve with a traditional wood fence.

Design

TYPES OF GATES

A gate is often the first thing to greet people as they approach an entry. Think carefully about the message you want your gate to send. The type of gate you choose depends on what you want the gate to do and the impression you want the gate to create.

Gates get more wear and abuse than any other part of a fence. They should be solidly built and attached with top-quality, heavy-duty hardware. Because the latch is the device people use to open and close the gate, it is often a focal point in the gate design.

Consider the look of your latch, as well as its mechanical operation—there are several different types; not all latches are suitable for every gate. You must either choose a latch that works with your gate design or adapt the gate design to work with a chosen latch. It's a good idea to choose latches and hinges for gates before you choose the gate itself. It is easier to design and build a gate to accommodate latches, hinges and the space between gate posts.

(above) **This intricately crafted double gate** *creates a formal, finished impression. To add to the elegance of the entryway, the gate is bordered with a lacy, custom-designed wrought-iron fence and is topped with a lovely iron arch.*

(left) **The enchanting design of this double gate** *enhances the entrance to this estate and brings classic charm to the setting. The capped, curved tops of the gate add shadow lines that enhance the visual effect of the evenly spaced, vertical boards.*

Photo courtesy of Walpole Woodworkers Inc.

44

The lacelike lattice design used on the fence top and gates *gives this entry a lighter, airier ambience. The open-weave design helps keep this large, solid fence from feeling too heavy and overbearing. A palatial pergola emphasizes the entrance and adds to the grandeur of this elegant gateway.*

STYLE OF GATES

The main function of a gate is to control access in and out of an area, and to guide visitors to the entrance. Front entry gates are often showpieces, but they can also be used to establish a welcome ambience in an entry area.

Gates can either match a fence or contrast with it. Focal point gates are designed to punctuate an entrance or highlight an entry area. Harmonious gates are designed to have a look that is similar to the fence, yet maintains some distinction of its own.

Discreet and concealed gates are designed to blend in as if they are part of the fence. They are sometimes built for security reasons, but more often they are designed this way because an obtrusive design would cause an unattractive break in the fence line.

Photo courtesy of California Redwood Association

(above) **This harmonious gate design** *maintains the smooth, clean look of the board fence. The delicate porthole and graceful arch over the door are subtle design elements that give this gate an air of distinction.*

(left) **This painted redwood gate** *is a focal point gate that highlights the point of entry and combines with an overhead arbor to create an outdoor foyer. The widely spaced lattice adds personality and a protective barrier that doesn't make the yard feel closed-in or isolated.*

This harmonious gate design blends *well with the rest of the fence and is quietly distinguished by a small panel of custom lattice work on each side of the door. Design details, such as the kickboard and rail cap on the fence and the extended posts of the gate, help to subtly indicate the entry area.*

FUNCTION OF GATES

A gate can either slide or swing open. Sliding gates are commonly used for driveways. They operate by sliding either on wheels or rollers attached to a track set in the ground. Your other option is a gate that swings open and closed. Your choice of the direction in which a gate swings will be influenced by both the location of the gate and the design of the fence.

The dimensions of your gate will depend on the height of the fence and the width of the walk, path or driveway it must span. The dimensions of a gate will also depend on how much you want the gate to stand out from the rest of the fence design.

When figuring the width of the gate opening, think about the type of traffic that will need to be able to pass through it. Will there be adequate clearance for mowers, wheelbarrows, garden furniture and other large items? Driveway gates should have enough clearance for trucks and cars to pass through without difficulty.

Photo courtesy of Walpole Woodworkers Inc.

*(left) A **delightful double gate** swings open to create a charming and inviting entry. The added detail of post caps in the middle of the gate gives it a unique quality.*

A swinging chain-link gate *establishes the entrance to this fenced-in area and is a relatively inexpensive option for safety or security fencing.*

Photo courtesy of Merchants Metals

A rooflike arbor sits over a swinging double gate, sheltering the entrance beneath it. The subtle design of the gate maintains the continuity of the look of the fence while the overhead arbor emphasizes this point of entry. A unique double door design uses two different gate widths. The smaller gate accommodates common foot traffic, while the larger gate allows the opening to be used for vehicles and other large items.

DECORATIVE ACCENTS

To add visual interest to an ordinary fence, or gate, you can dress it up with any number of decorative touches, such as a detailed fence or post top. The top of the fence is one of the first features people actually notice on a fence. No matter how simple or ornate the design of the fence is, the top edges and post tops are prominent aesthetic elements and among the most vividly memorable details about a fence or gate.

If you have an ordinary board fence, there are a number of tricks you can use to enhance its appeal. The fence top can be beveled in a long sweeping curve, giving the fence a scalloped look. Or, the tops of the boards can be cut in a special style to add a certain aesthetic feel to the fence. For example, the boards can be cut on a clean, straight line, or they can be given a special shape, such as a rounded or tulip shape.

*A **grand entrance** is created by this elaborate brick fence and ornamental iron gate. Sphere-shaped post tops accentuate the corners of this enclosure and even larger sphere-shaped pillar tops denote the entrance and complement the elaborate design. The top of the fence is accentuated with decorative edge brick, which has been turned vertically to create an effective visual contrast to the rest of the fence. A corner planting area fits into this fancy setting quite nicely.*

(above) **These whimsical gabled roofs** *are an example of the way decorative details play a prominent part in the overall influence of a fence. The roofed sections of the stepped fence are alternated with sections of small vertical boards to create a structure of amazing originality.*

(left) **The circular cutouts** *in this perky picket design create a unique variation of the classic picket fence. Altering the shape of the pickets is one way to create a fence that expresses an individual style.*

51

DECORATIVE ACCENTS FOR FENCES

Another way to accessorize fences and gates is with creative treatments of posts and fence tops. Posts can be extended to rise above the top stringers of the fence, or they can reach even higher to support a special border. One idea for a top border for a fence consists of a series of open frames. Other options include using a unique fill, such as lattice, attached at a contrasting diagonal. An extra-wide trim piece can be used to top the edge of a fence, or you can use a small attractive arbor to create a charming type of fence top.

Artistic treatments of fence posts can dress up a dull fence or gate. You can purchase prefabricated post caps that attach to your fence posts, or you can have them made. Some of the most common variations of post caps include diamond-shaped, round, pointed and beveled.

The largest, most noticeable part of a fence or gate is the face. A decorative panel or a window cut into the face will give a fence or gate a unique and custom appeal. For an easy fence upgrade, alternate panels of vertical and horizontal boards to create a checkerboard pattern on the frame side of a fence. Plants are always an easy way to add a colorful accent to a plain, ordinary fence.

Photo courtesy of California Redwood Association

Alternating boards with dog-eared shaped tops *with straight-topped boards adds an interesting visual effect to an otherwise ordinary fence design. An ornamental wrought-iron gate and an overhead pergola add to the appeal of the fence and enhance the enchanting grace of the gate.*

(above) **Custom woodworking** *and painted wood accents add an artistic touch to this formal-looking board fence. The unique creative treatment turns an ordinary outdoor structure into an artistic expression.*

(left) **Decoratively shaped boards** *enhance the traditional flavor of this pretty picket fence.*

DECORATIVE ACCENTS FOR GATES

Hinges are an easy way to add a decorative accent to a gate. They should be heavy enough to support the gate's weight and be able to withstand frequent use. Outdoor gate hinges should be made of a weather-resistant material, such as cadmium, zinc or galvanized metal. There are four basic types of hinges that are used on gates. They include bolt-hook-and-eye, butt, t- and strap hinges, and are available in several sizes and shapes. The bolts or screws used to attach the gate must be large and strong enough to hold the hinges to the gate. Three hinges are better than two. Heavy gates may require four hinges.

Photo courtesy of Walpole Woodworkers Inc.

Unique ball-and-chain hardware *serves as a creative counterbalance for closing the gate on this traditional white picket fence. This interesting hardware feature was an innovation of the nineteenth century, and is still in use today.*

(left) **Contrasting black hardware** *adds an interesting visual element to this grand entry gate.*

(right) **Ornamental fence and gate hardware** *is available in a variety of colors, shapes, sizes and styles. The type you choose will influence the type of fence or gate design you decide to use.*

A PORTFOLIO OF
FENCE
&
GATE
IDEAS

DEFINING BOUNDARIES

Installing a border fence around the perimeter of your property is a traditional and effective way to give your yard physical and visual definition. A fence and gate serve as reminders that the yard and house are both integral parts of the outdoor setting, and the right boundary fence and gate will link them together into a visual whole.

Establishing a perimeter fence will also simplify outdoor planning, and bring a sense of order to your property, much in the same way a frame complements a painting. Thoughtfully placing gates in logical spots will help you manage foot traffic. Arranging your yard in this way makes it easier to plan special areas for gardens, patios and other outdoor activities.

Fences and gates also distinguish your home from others that surround it, and the materials and styles used determine the kind of impression that is projected. A fence should work in harmony with the surrounding landscape and also with the neighborhood in general.

A wide choice of styles is available to help you decide the look and feel you want. A wood or vinyl picket fence and an ornamental iron fence may serve the same physical function, but each will evoke different emotions in people. Gates can range from stately entrances to nondescript, utilitarian entryways. Defining your house and surrounding yard with the right fence and gate style will bring a pleasing sense of completeness and order to your home.

The visual rhythms of this boundary fence harmonize nicely with the surrounding deck and give definition to this outdoor area. Surrounding trees and plants provide a lush and soothing texture.

(right) **A spacious outdoor recreation center** *is sheltered from strong winds by a lattice screen fence. Since the activity area is located in the corner of this lot, the lattice and nearby trees work together to provide privacy without totally blocking the view of those relaxing by the hot tub or surrounding deck.*

(below) **This attractive privacy fence** *borders the narrow walkway between properties and effectively blocks out unwanted views. Various plants find a home along the base of the fence and help soften the atmosphere.*

Photo courtesy of California Redwood Association

Photo courtesy of Milt Charno & Assoc., Inc.

(left) **A delightful backyard** is bordered and protected by a functional, unassuming perimeter fence. In the foreground, an additional fence provides a safe partition between the pool area and the rest of the property. Both fences combine with other landscaping elements like planters, railings and retaining walls to unite different areas into an enjoyable whole.

(below) **This picket design,** with its stately vertical lines, is a simple, assertive divider between the colorful garden and stone footpath on one side, and the lush trees and rolling meadow beyond.

Photo courtesy of Champlain Stone, Ltd.

(right) **The louvered panels** *of this beautiful fence offer just the right amount of privacy and solitude. This fence style affords a partial view of what lies beyond, yet clearly separates the hardwood deck from the adjoining property.*

(inset) **A low brick fence** *features a variety of shapes and patterns, and provides a defining backdrop for the garden area next to it. Separating two distinct types of landscape, this fence style blends in nicely between them.*

Photo courtesy of Brick Institute of America

Photo courtesy of California Redwood Association

Photo courtesy of Idaho Cedar Sales, Troy, ID

(left) **A secluded pool and deck** are sheltered from the nearby forest by a light louvered fence. The materials and design that were chosen allow this fence to quietly blend in with the natural surroundings, yet still provide the right amount of definition for this activity area.

(below) **The look and feel** of a country corral comes to this suburban backyard with the help of a simple split-rail fence. Sturdy cedar rails are mortised into the posts, and a matching gate preserves the overall look.

CONTROLLING CLIMATE

The fun of enjoying the outdoors is sometimes hampered by elements like excess wind, the unrelenting heat and glare from overhead sun, or loud, jarring noise from nearby traffic. Placing the right kind of fencing in strategic areas around your yard is an effective way to reduce these unwanted factors, and allow you to get the most from the outdoors.

For reducing daytime heat and sunlight, a breezy latticework fence will bring a comfortable degree of shade to a play area or sitting nook. It produces a diffuse shade that is easy on the eyes, but will allow enough light through for nearby plant life. Vertical louvered fences also restrict the amount of sun and wind that passes through them.

Putting fencing around an outdoor cooking or eating area can help reduce wind gusts that could tip drinks and plates. If you have a large yard, the type of perimeter fence you choose can determine how much wind sweeps through the area. The fence style most effective for reducing wind is not a solid wall, but one that lets a small amount of air pass through, like a lattice design or a board-and-slat pattern, and breaks a strong wind into a light breeze.

If street noise is a concern, the best bet is a solid wall that is as high as building codes will allow. A board-on-board pattern, with boards joined tightly together, can give an interesting surface that reduces noise and also shelters the yard, making the spot seem even more tranquil.

Decorative cement blocks *help this bold perimeter fence filter excess sunlight and break up gusts of wind before they enter the yard.*

Photo courtesy of Western Wood Products Association

(left) **This charming retreat** has a fence comprised of offset boards with a lattice top that occludes outside views while preserving an open, inviting atmosphere. The fence pattern provides shade on hot summer days, and allows soft breezes in to cool guests.

(below) **Slow down the wind** but keep the sun with this light gridwork of painted wood. Though this pattern is comprised of mostly empty space, the lattice provides enough resistance to break up wind, and the white color helps the fence stand out visually against the surrounding trees.

Photo courtesy of Walpole Woodworkers Inc.

(right) **A traditional picket fence,** *with gently curving tops and pickets placed closely together, will temper blowing winds, and in autumn will prevent fallen leaves from scattering.*

(right) **Outdoor snacks are safe** *from wind bursts with a fine lattice screen to soften breezes. Narrowly spaced slats also offer privacy from neighbors.*

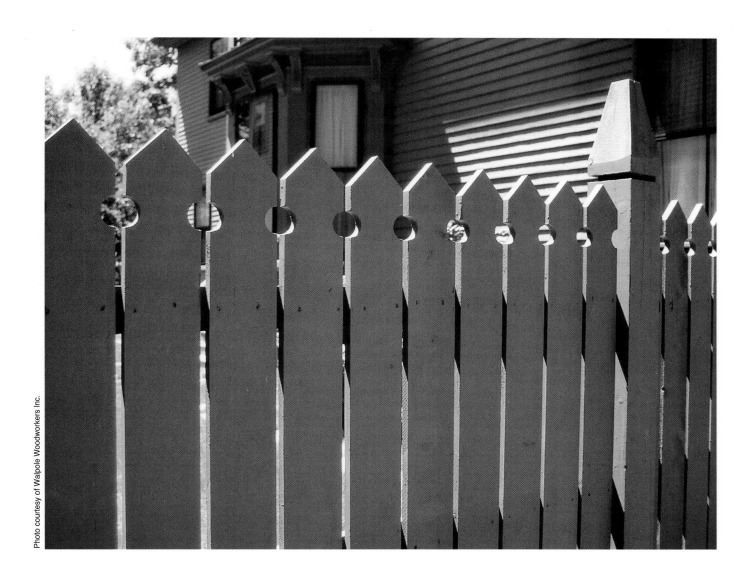

(above) **Tall, tightly spaced pickets** *block wind gusts and afternoon sun, and can help create a shady, relaxing area for dining or socializing. In situations like this, using wide pickets will be most efficient for blocking the elements and creating privacy.*

(right) **This substantial fence** *of red brick helps block out nearby traffic, while still seeming friendly and neighborly. This fence also provides a safe, protective barrier for young children, and peace of mind for parents.*

(above) **This fence and gate style** *features stepped sections that combine a solid board pattern below with narrow pickets on top, resulting in a decorative yet imposing barrier. Finials on the post tops soften the overall look and designate the gate entrance.*

(right) **Tall fences like this one** *are most effective for providing shade and shelter from wind. The louvered panels in this fence help scatter gusty winds, yet still provide a gorgeous view of the surrounding hills.*

PROVIDING PRIVACY & SECURITY

Fences and gates add privacy, which is a welcome commodity in our fast-paced society. Fencing around pools, picnic spots and sunbathing areas shelters users from the impact of the outside world and allows you to relax and enjoy yourself without distractions.

A solid fence wall will afford the most privacy. Designs range from basic to intricate, so you can find a style that's as beautiful as it is functional. Privacy fences should generally be built as high as local building codes allow. When planning for maximum privacy for a particular area, keep in mind sight lines from neighbors' upper-story windows and outdoor decks.

Many styles break up the view without totally blocking it out. A post-and-board pattern, with boards closely spaced but not touching, will filter the light passing through and still provide an effective barrier from unwanted views.

Ornamental iron fences may simply dissuade intruders by their look, but if security is a priority, then high chain-link or metal-mesh fences are hard to beat. They are effective and relatively inexpensive, with several unassuming styles available. Vinyl or wood slats can be inserted through the links to increase privacy.

Gates are potentially the weakest point of a fence, and can be strengthened with a variety of locks and reinforced hinges. Gates are also easily integrated with home security equipment like intercoms and electronic locks to help restrict entry and increase peace of mind.

*A **white screen** and arbor create a sitting area at one end of this impressive recreational area and offer protection from overhead sunlight. The redwood railing lining the edge of the overhanging deck provides safety and reassurance.*

(left) **For security and protection,** *this beautiful redwood gate is hard to beat. The capped posts bring a subtle touch of distinction to this functional, simple design.*

(below) **An ornamental iron fence,** *with pointed picket tips, provides an effective, imposing barrier in this heavily wooded area.*

(left) Diagonal boards
*identify the entrance gate of
this solid fence, which provides
safety and seclusion. A large
decorative arbor made of thick
timber beams reinforces the
aura of strength and durability.
Passing through this gate gives
friends and guests the feeling of
entering a secure fortress.*

Photo courtesy of Walpole Woodworkers Inc.

(above) **This sturdy gate,** *with its clean, smooth lines and supporting stone columns, announces with strength and reserve the formal entry to this secluded estate.*

(right) **Providing privacy** *and establishing a secure, attractive border, this tall fence is stepped to match the gentle incline along the property line. The lattice top gives this substantial fence a decorative edge, and makes it seem less massive.*

ENHANCING THE AMBIENCE

Fences and gates, aside from their functions as barriers and entryways, often are incorporated as landscaping tools. They provide practical ways for establishing ambience, organizing areas in your yard and for shaping outdoor atmospheres. Fencing styles can unify an outdoor design theme by creating a visual link between various areas of your yard, like decks and pool areas, or patios and gardens. Or several different fence designs can be used to highlight separate areas, and give each its own special identity.

By placing fencing around activity areas, you can divide a large yard into smaller, more manageable sections. This makes it easier to plan additional landscaping elements like flower beds, planters, retaining walls and sitting areas.

The variety of fencing styles and materials available can help you create different moods. Stately brick, warm redwood, and traditional painted cedar are just a few of your options. Let the natural features of your land and your sense of design inspire your imagination.

A fence gate fulfills the obvious need of an entryway through a fence, but gates also provide a great opportunity for deciding what kind of greeting you wish to offer. A gate can draw attention to itself and become an anchoring focal point for the surrounding space. Or if the fence itself is particularly ornate, the gate can simply serve as a subtle break in the structure to enter through, that when closed again seamlessly maintains the flow of the surrounding fence.

The redwood in this fence *provides the perfect background texture and color for a beautiful display of carefully manicured plant life. The spacing of the boards allows a glimpse of the trees beyond, increasing the visual effect.*

(right) **The square lattice pattern** *in this low perimeter fence echoes the architectural style of the windows and overall profile of the house it surrounds. Vines partially covering the fence team up with a variety of shrubs and plants to create a lush visual delight from both within and without.*

Photo courtesy of California Redwood Association

A designer variation combining both a board-and-rail and a lattice fence results in this unique and interesting design. The long, open fence quietly follows this ordered display of flowers, lending visual support while granting an unobstructed view of the surrounding flora.

(inset) *A simple side gate* receives an extra dash of excitement with this tall decorative arbor. The embellishment of the gate helps announce its location.

(right) **The decorative lattice** top of this fence is constructed of thick, heavy pieces of wood, which provide the perfect amount of visual substance to this light, airy design. The fence is a prominent element in this landscaping arrangement. It stands out against its dense surroundings, yet complements and supports the nearby trees and dazzling flowers.

Photo courtesy of California Redwood Association

(right) **A rugged garden area** is surrounded by this tall board-on-board fence. The amber color, varied texture and bold design of the fence help establish the garden's mood. The height of the fence also blocks outside views and allows those inside to enjoy the garden without distraction.

Photo courtesy of Brick Institute of America

Photo courtesy of California Redwood Association

(above) **A curved nook** *in this distinguished brick fence cradles a favorite garden statue. The alternating solid and open sections of the fence create a natural rhythm, and provide a dignified border for a beautiful bed of flowers.*

An overhead pergola announces the grand entrance of this high estate fence, and imparts a welcome yet exclusive feeling to this gateway. The bold design stands out against the towering trees in the background, and the curve of the gate adds a pleasing geometric contrast to the straight lines and right angles of the fence and pergola.

An ornate cap and finial *grace the top of this column, signifying a break in this Colonial-style fence. An antique lantern box lights the way after sunset and maintains the formal setting.*

(above) **A traditional picket fence** *completes the small-town, turn-of-the-century look of this charming New England home.*

(right) **The simple, bold lines** *of this garden entryway possess a strong, comforting appeal that acts as an invitation to the natural garden area beyond. The richness of the wood is enhanced by a colorful array of flowers and plants.*

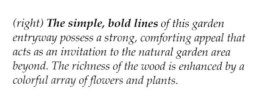

LIST OF CONTRIBUTORS

We'd like to thank the following companies for providing the photographs used in this book:

Bachman's Landscaping Service
800-222-4626
www.bachmans.com

Brick Institute of America
703-620-0010
www.brickinfo.org

California Redwood Association
888-CALREDWOOD
www.calredwood.org

Champlain Stone, Ltd.
518-623-2902
www.champlainstone.com

Country Estate Fence
800-445-2887
www.countryestate.com

CROSS VINYLattice
800-521-9878
www.crossvinyl.com

Gilbert & Bennett
203-544-8323

Idaho Cedar Sales, Inc.
208-835-2161

Merchants Metals
713-876-0080

Milt Charno & Associates, Inc.
414-475-1965

Monumental Iron Works
800-229-5615
www.fenceonline.com

Real Wood Products
541-689-8195

Southern Pine Marketing Council
504-443-4464
www.southerpine.com

Stanley Hardware
800-337-4393
www.stanleyhardware.com

Superior Aluminum Products, Inc.
www.superioraluminum.com

TCT Landscaping
805-688-3741

Walpole Woodworkers, Inc.
508-668-2800
www.walpolewoodworkers.com

Western Wood Products Association
503-224-3930
www.wwpa.com

© Copyright 1996
Creative Publishing international, Inc.
18705 Lake Drive East
Chanhassen, Minnesota 55317
1-800-328-3895
www.creativepub.com
All rights reserved

Printed by Quebecor World
10 9 8 7 6 5 4 3

President/CEO: Michael Eleftheriou
Vice President/Publisher: Linda Ball
Vice President/Retail Sales & Marketing:
    Kevin Haas

Author: Home How-To Institute™
Creative Director: William B. Jones
Associate Creative Director: Tim Himsel
Art Director: Gina Seeling
Group Executive Editor: Paul Currie
Managing Editor: Carol Harvatin
Copy Editor: Janice Cauley
Contributing Editor: Andrew Sweet
Vice President of Photography & Production:
    Jim Bindas
Production Coordinator: Laura Hokkanen

Library of Congress
Cataloging-in-Publication Data
Portfolio of fence & gate ideas.
    p. cm.

ISBN 0-86573-992-7 (softcover)
1.Fences. 2. Gates.
I. Cy DeCosse Incorporated.
NA8390.P58 1996
717—dc20 96-18889
CIP

Front cover photo of redwood gate and
fence courtesy of California Redwood
Association.

Back cover photos courtesy of Walpole
Woodworkers, Inc.